THE PERSONAL
BRAND BIBLE FOR
AMBITIOUS WOMEN

About the Author

Marielle Legair is a communications strategist, speaker and founder of Women Who Influence - a personal branding and publicity firm for female entrepreneurs.

With over a decade's international experience building brand reputation campaigns for some of the world's most renowned agencies, firms and blue chip companies, Marielle's work for her portfolio of clientele has captured global audiences' attention through top tier media channels including BBC, Bloomberg, Financial Times and Forbes.

She hosts personal branding masterclasses in New York and London, whilst being a speaker-of-choice for Yale University, New York University and KPMG on PR and entrepreneurship.

Born and raised in the UK, Marielle moved to New York in 2012 and used the personal branding strategies she teaches her clients to get established.

Visit: www.womenwhoinfluence.club for more information.

The Personal Brand Bible for Ambitious Women

FEATURING SUCCESS SECRETS FROM SIX-FIGURE TRAILBLAZERS

Marielle Legair

ISBN: 1974444600
ISBN 13: 9781974444601

DEDICATION

---

*To all the ambitious women out there who never let fear get
in the way of sharing their gifts and talents with the world.
Keep shining bright.*

You were born with potential.
You were born with goodness and trust.
You were born with ideals and dreams.
You were born with greatness.
You were born with wings.
You are not meant for crawling, so don't.
You have wings.
Learn to use them and fly.

—Rumi

Contents

Preface

If you are a woman with big dreams, this book is for you.

In case you haven't noticed, the world of work as we know it is changing fast. *Forbes* estimates that by 2020, 50 percent of the US workforce will freelance in some capacity. Therefore, the need to become known for your expertise is crucial. A recognizable personal brand will lead to more opportunities, whether you're looking to increase sales in your business, climb the corporate ladder or land a new job. You cannot afford to blend in; you must do everything you can to stand out.

I regularly meet women who want to raise their profile at work or as an entrepreneur but, for whatever reason, don't feel comfortable doing so or don't know where to begin. I hope this book provides valuable insight and inspiration to you.

You will learn the secret sauce to building a personal brand from in-depth interviews with five massively successful women. These are the gems I wish I had known when I started my career. I think I have achieved a lot. But had I known all that is shared here, I'd have long built my empire, and I would be sitting on a beach in the Caribbean sipping on a rum punch right now. Nevertheless, I'm confident these practical tips will equip you with the tools to take your career or business to the next level.

If you find this book useful, share it with your girlfriends to inspire and uplift them!

Much love,
Marielle

PART 1

BUILDING YOUR PERSONAL BRAND

Regardless of age, regardless of position, regardless of the business we happen to be in, all of us need to understand the importance of branding. We are CEOs of our own companies: Me, Inc. To be in business today, our most important job is to be head marketer for the brand called You.

—Tom Peters, management guru.

Now Is the Time

With so many resources at our fingertips, there has never been a better time for you to become known for your expertise. Whether you are a student, have a nine-to-five, or are an entrepreneur, you are always selling your ideas. People want to do business with people with whom they can build a rapport, not faceless corporations. Gone are the days where you spend twenty-five years at a firm and receive a gold watch at retirement. The average person today is estimated to change jobs every two to three years; therefore, building a recognizable personal brand is key.

Reputation Is Everything

You have to put in work to become known for your expertise. You want to be the one whose name comes up in conversation as the go-to person in your industry. Of course, this doesn't happen overnight. There are strategies you can begin to develop. Perennial best-selling author, Malcolm Gladwell in his book *Outliers* says ten thousand hours of "deliberate practice are needed to become world-class in any field." Daniel Priestley, an Australian entrepreneur and author, says there are "key people of influence" in every industry. Their names come up in conversations, they attract more opportunities, and they earn more money. How great would it be to become one of those people?

As an employee, think of it this way: If you were to lose your current job tomorrow, how easy would it be to demonstrate your expertise to a new employer?

For entrepreneurs, a personal brand is even more crucial, in my opinion. Having your customers and clients know, like, and trust what you are selling is the only way to grow.

Long story short: reputation is everything. Consciously manage your reputation, or someone else will.

Steps to Building Your Personal Brand

Get Clear

Identify what you want to be known for. The more specialized you can become, the better. There are riches in the niches, after all. A publicist working with female coaches running six-figure businesses is far more specific than a publicist who works with entrepreneurs. Your target clients will have an easier time finding you when your message clearly speaks to them.

If you're struggling to define your niche, think about what your friends or colleagues say is your greatest strength. Or imagine yourself walking into a bookstore: Which sections do you generally gravitate toward (self-help, business, finance, cooking, etc.)? This should give you an indication of what you're most passionate about.

Master Your Craft

What skills must you develop to eventually become an expert in your niche? As an entrepreneur, you might need skills like public speaking and website development. These skills will help you confidently sell your ideas, in person and online.

Claim Your Domain Name

A personal website showcasing your portfolio of work should form a key part of your online brand. People will google you after meeting you, so make sure your best work is readily on display.

Create a Unique Brand Identity

A professional and authentic visual identity is fundamental to creating a unique personal brand in the digital age. The online world is noisy, with competitors sprouting up in your industry daily; therefore, it's crucial to stand out so you're not easily forgotten.

"If you are marketing yourself as an expert on a subject, your brand identity is what your audience thinks of you as an individual. This typically involves the creation of a name accompanied by a series of visual imagery and verbal messages," says Gregory V. Diehl, author, podcaster, and coach.

This includes design, colors, fonts, photography, and customer service. It's the overall look and feel you convey to your audience.

What identifies your goods or service as distinct from those of others in your niche? Take some time to do a thorough brand audit.

Key considerations include

- your company name and tagline;
- your logo, signature graphics, and color scheme;
- sounds and styles that characterize your company;
- your tone of voice and messaging; and
- the emotions you want your current and prospective clients to feel.

If branding is not your strong point, please outsource this to a professional designer. Your website should not look like a five-year-old designed it.

Be You. Be Authentic.

The identity you have established for yourself online must be congruent with who you really are. That way there will be no surprises! Be yourself: professional and genuine. No point trying to be anyone else. Focus on the unique strengths that make you you. This will endear you to your audience and quickly build a rapport. Tell your story. Let people into your world. You can decide how much you reveal, but remember real connections matter.

Share Your Vision

No matter how great you are at what you do, it means nothing if no one knows who you are and what you do.

"Market the bejesus out of your brand—to customers, colleagues, and your virtual network of associates," says management guru Tom Peters.

People with a large public persona are often good at sharing their vision with the world. Oprah Winfrey's mission when she started her TV show was to be a teacher and to be known for inspiring her students to be more than they thought they could be.

Similarly, Sara Blakely the world's youngest self-made woman billionaire often talks about her mission: "To help women feel great about themselves and their potential." Her motivation for creating Spanx stemmed from the need to help women feel more comfortable in their undergarments.

Think about how you can share your vision with the world.

Build Confidence

"Do one thing every day that scares you," Eleanor Roosevelt said. We increase confidence that way. Try it. Over time you'll have built that muscle. You'll become much less fearful of obstacles. I was afraid to travel alone, so to overcome that fear I went on a solo trip to Rio de Janeiro. It was a life-changing experience that has undoubtedly given me the confidence to face bigger life challenges, like relocating from London to New York.

Solo travel may not be your thing, but think about other goals that will really stretch you. It takes a certain level of confidence to put yourself out there. Take one step at a time. As long as you're challenging yourself each day, you'll build a bank of confidence in no time.

Surprise and Delight

Under promise and over deliver. Always. Never be the woman who talks a good game but doesn't deliver results. It's a surefire way to lose respect. Fast. Speak less. Put your head down and work. Don't be afraid to share your successes. Remember: It's not bragging if it's true!

Benefits of a Personal Brand

- Establish credibility in your niche.
- Increase earning potential.
- Find a better job with more prospects.
- Win more clients.
- Have people pitch you rather than the other way around.

- Work fewer hours and stop trading time for money.
- Build a global tribe of loyal fans.

Your Network Is Your Net Worth

A solid network is crucial to building your personal brand. Always try to meet people in person if possible. As convenient as the online world is, the power of in-person chemistry is far greater and is the quickest way to develop a deep and meaningful relationship. Even if no new business comes of it, you still might make a new friend. I've had multiple job offers, consulting gigs, fancy dinners, and free access to expensive conferences simply by being connected to the right people.

Moving to New York from London meant I had to build a new network quickly. New Yorkers are generally more forthcoming than Londoners, which took some getting used to. I forced myself to attend at least two or three networking events per week.

Developing a way to assess people quickly was key. When meeting people for the first time, I use the following criteria:

1. Do I get a good vibe about this person? Do they look me in the eye when introducing themselves? Do they have a firm handshake?
2. Does this person seem genuinely interested in others? Or do they just talk about themselves? Have

you ever met a person for the first time who gives a fifteen-minute monologue about their life? I have. I was bored to tears. Upon meeting self-obsessed types, make your excuses and leave the conversation.

3. Does the person seem happy? I'm an optimist. I love to be around people who share the same zest for life as I do. I quickly lose interest in lethargic, miserable people. You know the type—everything seems to go wrong in their life, and it's never their fault. Energy is contagious; be selective with whom you spend time.

You may already have your own criteria. Either way, it's good to proactively build a vibrant network of people of all ages, ethnicities, and backgrounds.

Distance yourself from "Debbie Downers"—negative personalities. "Stop hanging around people who don't want to win," as serial entrepreneur Gary Vaynerchuk says. You'd be surprised how much more motivated you become by hanging around doers who encourage and push you outside of your comfort zone.

Plan Ahead

Find out who is attending the networking event ahead of time. Arrive early, or at least on time, so you're not flustered. If you're going to a popular event, get there early enough to get a seat at a table so you're in a good position to contribute to the conversation.

Don't Bitch

Never speak ill of others. You'll only come across as a Petty Patty. People will wonder what you'll say about them. Plus, you never know who knows who. Six degrees of separation is even smaller with social media.

Go Alone

Attending an event by yourself will force you to talk to more people. As daunting as it may seem at first, you're there to meet new contacts so use the alone time as motivation to meet someone new.

Speak with Intention

Know what you want to say and what you want to get out of each conversation. Check the news before arriving so that you're well informed about current events.

Approach Odd Numbers

If you see two people in the room having an in-depth conversation, leave them to it. They may be annoyed at you for interrupting. Find a group with an opening and speak to the person who isn't engaged in conversation with someone else.

Stay in Touch

We've all had a friend who disappears off the face of the earth when she gets a new boyfriend and magically reappears when they break up. Networking is similar. Don't be that person. Regularly stay in touch with the contacts you make. Even if you send an article that may be of interest, a quick text to say hello, or a holiday card. Any of these are better than just making contact when you need something.

Don't Waste Your Pretty

First impressions count. Anyone who says looks are not important is lying. Looking well put together may not be the be-all and end-all, but it will take you further than looking a hot mess. It's all part of your personal brand. There's a reason successful people spend time on their appearances. They are mindful of their diet and pay close attention to their physical, mental, and spiritual well-being.

Rest

Sleep is so underrated. I'm weary of people who brag about only needing a few hours of sleep a night. Nothing compensates for a good night's sleep to ensure you're operating at your best. Set an alarm at night the way you would to wake up to remind yourself to start getting ready for bed. It's easy to waste time surfing the Internet aimlessly into the early hours when you could be getting some rest.

Spirituality

With so much going on in the world, we all need an outlet. Carve out the first few minutes of your day for your own quiet time. Whether it be meditation, yoga, or journaling, choose something that works for you. If it means waking up a little earlier, then do that. You'll feel much more centered and better able to deal with any challenges that arise during the day. Invest in a journal to write down your thoughts and ideas before bed or as soon as you wake up in the morning. It's incredibly cathartic. Building a brand takes a ton of time and focused energy. The more you can build a resilient emotional state, the more effective you will be.

You Are What You Eat

Your ability to focus and perform is heavily influenced by what you eat. Start the day with a healthy, protein-rich, and low-carb breakfast to preserve your energy. Stay hydrated throughout the day by keeping a two-liter bottle of water on your desk. This will help you feel less groggy and more energized.

Get Movin'!

Move your body in some kind of way for a minimum of thirty minutes each day. Yoga, jumping jacks, or high-intensity interval training, for example, will boost your mood.

Invest in Your Wardrobe

You don't need to spend a ton of money to look good. But at least invest in quality basics. A crisp white shirt, a nice handbag, quality leather shoes, and a smart black dress. You never know what last-minute meetings will crop up. You want people to want you on their team.

Build Your Personal Brand Checklist

Consider these statements when building your personal brand:

☐ I am clear on what I want to be known for.

☐ I have created a powerful pitch to explain what I do to others.

☐ I have a professional website.

☐ I have created a unique, professional brand identity.

☐ I network well and often.

☐ I eat a healthy breakfast and stay hydrated throughout the day.

☐ I move my body each day (cardio, yoga or dance, etc.).

PART 2

AWESOME WOMEN CRUSHIN' IT

*And the day came when the risk
to remain tight in a bud was more
painful than the risk it took to blossom.*

—Elizabeth Appell, Award-winning
novelist, playwright, and screenwriter.

SAMMY AKI

To establish myself as an authority, I used my luxury sector knowledge as well the PR experience gained working with the oldest wedding dress brand in Europe to pitch my story to journalists and bloggers.

Founder of the Groom Style Consultant.

Carving Out a Niche as a Menswear Consultant

I've been working in the luxury menswear sector for over fifteen years. I started on Jermyn Street in London, the traditional home of men's shirting and accessories. I transitioned to styling celebrities and magazine shoots for the likes of *Esquire* and *GQ* and to producing menswear events for the tailoring houses of Savile Row. After years of working with companies that design, create, and promote the best clothing, I developed extensive knowledge of the menswear industry.

My experience working on the shop floor with those who actually wore the end product proved invaluable to what I do today. During this time, I often noticed men coming in looking for six wedding suits with matching ties, last minute and in a panic, not knowing what to do. They'd want a custom-made wedding suit, but they did not realize that the process takes three months.

I saw a gap in the market to better enable men. There were all these services for women to get their dream dress and enjoy the process, but not much was available to men.

To establish myself as an authority, I used my knowledge of the luxury sector as well the PR experience I gained working with the oldest wedding dress brand in Europe to pitch my story to journalists and bloggers. I secured press coverage in the *Metro*, a free newspaper handed to commuters in London and other major cities across England. They ran a full-page spread about my career with a photo of me in it! The feature gave me exposure to a wider audience and the boost I personally needed at the early stage of venturing out on my own. I received so many new business inquiries from those in the industry and from potential clients and other journalists who had read my story.

I have always wanted to understand the industry from as many angles as possible. I hope having broad experience will now better enrich the teams I build going forward. Today I'm applying my business skills and trying to manage myself. Every day is different, which keeps it interesting. It's about learning from people around you and expanding on those skills. Those people can be any age from eight to eighty years old.

My greatest achievement has been carving out a niche in the luxury industry for men getting married when the market was nonexistent. Obviously, men can go to their tailor to get something made or go to a department store. But when I was starting out, there was nothing specific to give men the full-on experience while preparing for their wedding. No one was focused on that market. I had to get brands on board and develop my own brand. It was amazing to get high-profile, world-renowned, and respected companies to work with me.

I was featured in two major publications. Early on in my career, I met Sarah Haywood, the author of *Wedding Bible*, the definitive guide to organizing a luxury wedding. She was updating the book and wanted us to work together. I was commissioned to write the grooms chapter, which had not previously been included in the first edition. I'm featured alongside exceptionally talented experts and craftspeople within the wedding industry, many of whom worked on the Duke and Duchess of Cambridge's wedding.

As an entrepreneur, it's sometimes a challenge to keep going, but I seem to thrive on the challenge. Relocating from London to New York in September 2016 meant I've had to take the time to rethink my business model and adapt my approach and tone. It's an opportunity to reassess and go forward.

"If you don't ask, you don't get" is the best piece of career advice I've received.

Think and Grow Rich by Napoleon Hill is the book that has most inspired my journey.

"Honesty is the best policy" is the mantra I live by.

My advice to anyone looking to build their personal brand:

1. Be true to yourself and be yourself.
2. Don't get overwhelmed with what others are doing. It's important to stay focused on your goals.
3. Build your tribe. Talk and share with others who are developing their companies at all stages. When I first started, I spent a lot of time working from home, which can be very isolating. It's important to manage your time and your relationships with your friends, making sure you are carving out downtime.

www.sammyaki.com
Instagram: @sammyaki

NANA DARKO

The ones who get ahead seem to be "present" in any given situation and have cultivated a solid network.

Lawyer and Oxford University Graduate.

Juggling a Successful Career as a Finance Lawyer and Motherhood

It was almost predetermined that I'd become a lawyer. From a young age, family members would always say that I argued a case well. Applying to study law was the most obvious thing. When I got to university, my eyes were opened to a life of law beyond what was shown on the TV. I realized that there is another side—an intellectual side of law—that to me is incredibly stimulating. Being at Oxford really broadened my horizons. I met people at corporate law firms, and I could see myself working within the profession.

I try not to become too specialized as that may limit my future career progression. Outside of my firm, the law is not divided up into nice little practice areas. Therefore, counterintuitive though it might sound to other professions, I believe that remaining as general as possible is the key to having a long-lasting legal career (especially if you go down the in-house legal/general counsel route).

I have gone out of my way to ensure I don't have a niche. Instead, I've focused on developing a breadth of practice across the leverage finance, restructuring, and insolvency spaces. This also helps with keeping me interested and intellectually stimulated. I'm really focused on being a good lawyer. When a client calls me, I want to be known as someone who gives sound and comprehensive advice. You only get that from working across multiple disciplines and transactions. I want to be a master of my craft. Therefore, for my own professional and personal development, I've tried to be as broad as possible.

I'm very aware of my strengths and weaknesses. Oratory has never been my thing. I love to talk, but I'm stronger on the analytical and research-based side. Hence, I thought the solicitor route made more sense for me. More than the drafting, negotiation, or advocacy skills you need to be a lawyer, to be an effective corporate solicitor takes a lot of the soft skills. Being liked and respected and someone people enjoy working with and for. The people I have known to excel and be successful in this game have not necessarily been the smartest academically. They have built a strong personal brand and displayed confidence.

I sought one-on-one coaching to help me build my personal brand more effectively. When I came up for promotion a few years ago, my mentor told me that, in terms of my work, no one would ever question it. But she asked, "Do people know who you are? Does everyone know what you are a capable of?" Her feedback got me thinking.

I've always made myself known in a social setting but not in a work setting. This is very common among ethnic minorities—I'm very much head down and focused on getting my work done. Naturally, as a black woman in a mainly white, corporate environment, people do know who I am because we're so rare. Unfortunately, people assume (because we generally look younger than we are) that you are more junior. As such, most of my coaching has been to bolster my image and my external profile rather than my technical capabilities.

The whole concept of being a minority, one of the few at Oxford, didn't bother me. I was more concerned with the change of moving out of London and losing the friends I'd had since childhood. I was never worried about Oxford, because I honestly never thought I would get in.

The interviews for Oxford are a real test of how much someone likes you. I've heard rumors of walking into the room and seeing the interviewer sit silently and throwing a tennis ball at a wall to provoke a response from you. Thankfully, I didn't have anything like that! I remember thinking, "Oh my God. My shirt is too tight" and "I wish I had chosen a better suit." The tutor who interviewed me was what most people would describe as a "weirdo." He wouldn't look me directly in the eye. He just said the first things that came to his head: "That's a silly thing to say, isn't it?" and "You must have read that in a silly book." and "State-school students always say things like that." But it didn't throw me; I just found him intriguing and, frankly, hilarious! I didn't feel I did particularly well during the interview, so getting a call just before Christmas telling me I'd been accepted was a major surprise.

Luckily, I haven't faced many huge setbacks during my career. Although juggling work in the city with being a mother has certainly been a challenge. Every day is a military operation. To-do lists, schedules, and limited twiddling of thumbs are key. Everything has to be super organized and preplanned or it simply does not work. You also have to learn to prioritize, delegate, and be assertive like never before. Having an amazing husband, fantastic childcare, and incredible familial support also helps (particularly when I'm working long hours or weekends or while on holiday).

"Make sure you're in the driver's seat of your career" is the best piece of career advice I've received.

"Time is how you spend your love" is the mantra I live by.

My mentors have been invaluable to me. I regularly seek advice and counsel from the wise people I have around me.

My advice to anyone looking to build their personal brand:

1. Try to be the most authentic version of you. If you try to be someone else, you'll get found out and tired.
2. Don't forget your morals and your integrity. Those are values you should not sacrifice. Ever.

3. Be patient. A personal brand is something that is built over time rather than overnight. People should focus more on working hard and doing good quality work; from that, a good personal brand follows.

Having a personal brand is just as important to employees as it is to entrepreneurs. It's really important to be visible as an employee. If you just blend in at a big law firm like Linklaters, the system is designed to ensure that people fall off at every obstacle. They start with an intake of 120 people, and of that number only one will make partner. The ones who survive are those most visible and who don't get worn out by the process, not necessarily the best. Those are the ones really out there and well networked. I can already identify the people in my peer group earmarked for partnership. They seem to be "present" in any given situation and have cultivated a solid network.

NATALIE DIVER

All day, all night I was learning. I worked so many hours every single day to learn about the business.

Creator of OMG Detox and CEO of Boss Babe.

Creating a Detoxing Beauty Blend and Running a Global Network for Millennial Women Entrepreneurs

I'd always wanted to have my own business. I got offered a corporate job, but I knew I wanted to travel. While traveling, I was having health issues with my stomach, so I began to pay more attention to nutrition. I found it impossible to get a healthy product that wasn't packed with sugar and chemicals. So I turned down the corporate job and decided to follow my passion of creating a healthy nutrition product. It took me a year to get my product launched. I have a business management background, but I had no knowledge of the nutrition industry. I was very picky about the product, so it took me a while.

I set up the Instagram account for OMG Detox five months before launching. That's when I really learned how to build a following on Instagram and how to market a brand. I had built a waiting list of customers before launching, which really helped expedite sales.

OMG Detox has always had a strong mission. We'll never promote a negative self-image. We're all about self-love and empowerment. Upon launching OMG Detox, I asked for testimonials. There are so many products out there, so testimonials are key. They've been really helpful in establishing the brand.

I've had to master so many new skills as a business owner. Instagram and Photoshop were all new to me. Plus, I had zero budget, so I had to be cost-efficient. As my business grows, I've had to learn softer skills, like how to delegate. Also, the operational side of my business, like working with retailers, has been a steep learning curve.

All day and all night, I was learning. I worked so many hours every single day to learn about the business. It was absolutely exhausting. I remember thinking so many times, "Is this even worth it?" The launch date kept getting pushed back, which was frustrating.

Mindset is everything in business. You can have a shitty day, but if you believe in yourself and keep going, you'll become stronger. Entrepreneurship is an emotional journey. Routines are really important. I have a meeting with myself each week. It may sound strange, but I block time out to assess where I'm going, what works well, and where I need to spend more time.

I work out every single day. Monday through Friday, no matter how busy I am. I believe that keeps your mind in a healthy place. When you're an entrepreneur, it's easy to let yourself go sometimes.

My proudest achievement is winning an award at the university I attended in recognition for my contribution to entrepreneurial projects and impacting others.

The best piece of career advice I've received came when I was deciding whether to go for the corporate job or to launch my business. Niyc Pidgeon (featured in this book) said, "What is the absolute worst that can happen? If you can handle the absolute worst thing, then go for it." So that's now how I make tough decisions.

These books have inspired my journey:

1. *How to Win Friends and Influence People*, by Dale Carnegie.
2. *The Four-Hour Workweek*, by Tim Ferriss. I've learned so much from him, especially about how to outsource certain parts of business. That's been really helpful.
3. *Elon Musk: Tesla, SpaceX, and the Quest for a Fantastic Future*, by Elon Musk. Musk's biography makes you realize that you have to keep going. He was close to losing everything but went against what people said.
4. *If You Have to Cry, Go Outside: And Other Things Your Mother Never Told You*, by Kelly Cutrone. She owns a PR company in New York. The book outlines what she's learned along the way. It's really inspiring. Anytime I'm feeling down, I read a page of that, and I feel like a badass.

"Just do it" is the mantra I live by.

I have several mentors. It's so helpful to have people who have done what I'm trying to do. Sometimes my mentors just give me advice. They are so important. I've learned to never be afraid to contact someone who can help me.

My advice to anyone looking to build their personal brand:

1. Get clear on your niche. What's your core message? What do you stand for? Also, what do you stand against? You have to be real. Find out who you need to appeal to.
2. Be relatable. Don't think you have to reinvent yourself fully; it's totally okay to look to those who inspire you for guidance.
3. Be consistent. If you're visible, then your branding needs to be coherent.

www.omgdetox.com
www.bossbabe.co
Instagram: @natalie.diver

NIYC PIDGEON

Get over the fear of being visible. Do it quickly.
Keep putting content out again and again.

Psychologist, global
success coach, and author.

Implementing Her Mission to Help One Million Women around the World Change Their Lives Using Positive Psychology by 2020

I've always wanted to run a business. I excelled academically in school. Initially, I wanted to be an engineer. When I was seventeen, I traveled to Australia with my partner at the time. He was a professional cricket player. During a visualization session his sports psychologist told him when on the cricket pitch, "Don't look around at the fielders. Instead, look for the gaps between the fielders." That was huge for me. It's so easy to focus on the obstacles and challenges, but if we focus on the opportunities and what we want to create, life is much better. I came back from Australia and changed my degree from engineering to sports psychology. Then I went on to do a master's degree in positive psychology. After studying I began to explore further the idea of working for myself.

I love to help women find their personal power through entrepreneurship, though I don't believe working for yourself is the endgame. Business ownership helps us develop in both a professional capacity and a personal capacity. I see a huge need for people to find empowerment and happiness.

My qualifications have helped me stand out in the coaching industry. While you don't need qualifications, having them helped me establish myself as an expert and an authority. I'm grateful to have taken the time to study. A small success hack that has helped me to stand in my power is to use my titles "positive psychologist" and "global success coach" in my marketing copy and e-mails.

Sharing content and adding value are essential. If you want to be known as a thought leader, you have to get comfortable sharing your expertise and knowledge. You have to be the person seen on social media as helping people develop and learn.

I used to be really scared of using video for my business. But it has helped me massively to connect with my audience. One of my weaknesses is probably being too raw, but it's much better to be authentic!

Online marketing is a core skill entrepreneurs need to master. I have four team members who manage a large amount of my online activity, but I'm glad to have learned that skill myself. I love looking at statistics and coming up with ideas and content. Breaking through fears is another area I've really had to master. People think it's just the launch of the business that is the fear.

Every single phase of growth requires a different mindset. You must face up to your fears, and you don't always know where they are going to come from. It's about understanding that as you grow, your earning potential increases based on the risks you're willing to take. You have to challenge yourself to learn to deal with those things.

My book deal with Hay House, one of the largest publishers of self-help, inspirational, and transformational books and products, and my being a United Nations (UN) Women's Ambassador for the United Kingdom are my greatest achievements to date. I'm working with the UN to help promote gender equality and end domestic violence against women. I've had a desire to be a UN ambassador for a while, but initially, I thought it was too big a goal to ever become possible. But then I reminded myself what I teach others: if you want to make something real, you have to start talking about it and own it.

I did a Facebook Live stream and mentioned the UN goal during it. I then got into talks with the woman who conceptualized the ONEBRACELET, an awesome orange bracelet created to raise awareness and empower women suffering from domestic violence around the world. It seemed like such a good fit and a natural progression. The messaging is aligned with my book as well, so I'm really pleased with the partnership.

I had a really difficult year in 2014. From that experience, I learned how to share more of myself and the value of sharing my story. The following year, I went to the Hay House Writer's Workshop. It was such a fantastic experience to learn from some of its best authors. I learned about book writing and submitted my proposal in November 2015. I then got a phone call in January 2016 letting me know that I had won the book-writing competition! That was just the beginning. Book writing takes a lot of energy; it's very personal. A lot of self-doubt comes up. It's a very big process.

Self-doubt is definitely one of the biggest challenges I've had to overcome. Most of the obstacles entrepreneurs experience are internal. People don't realize this. They think it's a skills gap that you can go out and learn. It's a lot more difficult if you're doubting yourself. Exhaustion is another challenge for me. I'm really good at saying yes to a lot of things. Self-care is something I teach because it's the one thing I need to learn most.

I start every day with a morning ritual. My ritual keeps me on track and is foundational to my success. I always start my day at five fifteen. I do gratitude and affirmations and work on my vision and goals. I then go to a cardio class at six o'clock. I'm ready to start the day by eight, feeling good. I work out every day. I'm also very big on health and nutrition. I know that if I didn't have a healthy diet, I'd fall down. I always have a weekly massage. I try to have a day off each week, but it doesn't always happen. For me, it's about carving out quiet time because I've got such a big community. It's good to find solace and shut out the world once in a while.

Here are the three best pieces of career advice I've received:

1. Be yourself.
2. Use your name for your business. The moment I began to do this it significantly transformed my business.

3.   Don't be afraid to tell your story.

These books have inspired my journey:

1.   *Mind Gym:* An Athlete's Guide to Inner Excellence by Gary Mack
2.   *Girlosophy*, an amazing coffee table book by Anthea Paul
3.   *Rich Dad Poor Dad* by Robert Kiyosaki because of how it changes your perspective on finance

"Our minds were born with wings to help us soar above reality" is the mantra I live by, taken from my book *Now Is Your Chance.*

I work with various mentors. They have been invaluable in terms of my self-belief as well as providing wisdom and expertise.

My advice to anyone looking to build their personal brand:

1.   Create a unique brand identity. Pick a color that you want to be associated with, one that resonates with you and your brand. When people meet me, they often say, "You're that girl in the pink dress." (I'm wearing a pink dress on the home page of my website.)
2.   Get over the fear of being visible. Do it quickly. You think everyone is looking at you, and they're not. So keep putting content out again and again.

3. Be authentic. The more you can be yourself, the better. You will eventually polarize your audience, which is a good thing. You will develop a loyal base of raving fans.

www.niycpidgeon.com
Instagram: @niycpidge

TONYA RAPLEY

While you're building your business.
You need to be everywhere your audience
turns. Your presence needs to be undeniable.

Founder and CEO of MyFabFinance.com,
a website dedicated to improving
millennial women's relationship
with money.

Building a Six-Figure Global Personal Finance Brand

There was a lack of millennial women of color in the personal finance industry. I felt we had older white women in the space but none who looked like me. I graduated from college at the height of the recession, and when I created My Fab Finance, there wasn't someone speaking from that perspective. Nor was there someone speaking directly to audiences who were dealing with the complexities of being a minority in the workplace and the ways it can impact their finances. I wanted to approach teaching personal finance from that point of view.

I took certain steps to establish myself as an authority in my niche. I got my certification as a financial education instructor because both of my degrees were social service oriented. I knew what I was talking about but wanted the credibility. I made sure I learned as much as I could about personal finance and how to create behavioral change.

Social media is a pleasant disrupter. I create content for social media to help people understand they are capable of changing their financial situation. Social media is the reason I've been able to secure all my television opportunities. Just yesterday, I had a call from a representative of a major television network who had googled me. It goes to show how important it is to own your space online. By showing up consistently and getting your name out there, you position yourself as an expert for upcoming stories or projects.

One specific skill I've developed as an entrepreneur is the ability to build and maintain good relationships. As a business owner, I deal with various personalities ranging from pleasant to unpleasant. I've had to learn not to take things personally and handle things objectively and with more grace. My technology learning curve is something I've focused on, too. I don't ever want to be in a position where I'm stuck if the freelancers or consultants I've hired aren't around to execute a task. I had to learn how to do certain things like Photoshop. I also have a better understanding of how my website works and how to code.

I launched My Fab Finance in January 2013. By October 2015 I was on the front cover of *Black Enterprise*, an American magazine aimed at the black business community. That was huge; it happened less than two years after starting my business. Recently, My Fab Finance was voted the best personal finance blog for women by the Plutus Foundation, the highest award issued by personal finance bloggers and professionals. I'm very clear about helping women, so I was very pleased to have my work recognized. Then I was named a Modern History Maker by TV One. The network wanted to position the story through the lens of trailblazing black women.

Toyota chose me to tell me the story of transitioning into entrepreneurship in their new #IDoTheNew campaign, which is about how I decided to live my life differently. It's a tremendous honor. I never thought I'd do a commercial.

Initially, I had to overcome my own blocks. I didn't grow up around a lot of entrepreneurs, so I often questioned if I was built to do this. There were a lot of doubts about whether I could create a business model. During the first month of working for myself, my biggest client, a high-profile celebrity, had a PR nightmare. I had to withdraw myself from the deal, which was a huge blow because I had based my business model on that revenue.

I thought I had everything figured out, and then everything was turned upside down. I developed ulcers. It was a mess. I then went on to become profitable in my first year, but having to terminate the deal with the celebrity was a setback. I had to go into myself. I pulled back for a month to sort through it and figure out my course of action. As a result of that, I'm now very cautious about any relationship I enter into. My integrity is everything. If I allow anything to compromise that, it compromises my brand. All money is not good money.

"Be kind to yourself" is the best piece of advice I've received. As an entrepreneur, I know it's very easy to get down on yourself and go into that tunnel of self-deprecation.

Just run your race. Everyone is going to have opinions about how you should manage your business. Just because something works for someone doesn't mean it will work for you. So it's really important to stay focused. Remember why you started. It's easy to get caught up in mentions and accolades, especially in the personal change space. Never forget why you started.

These books have inspired my journey:

1. *The Alchemist* by Paulo Coelho. I love this book so much. I read it four years before I started My Fab Finance. It dramatically changed my life in New York. It was my primer on the law of attraction and understanding the ability we have to cocreate our reality.
2. *The Power of Habit* by Charles Duhigg has given me so much insight into how we create habits.
3. *Feel It Real* by Denise Coates. I'm very spiritual. This book is about how to program your thinking and change your vibration so that you approach things from a higher level. The book emphasizes the importance of thinking about opportunities and possibilities rather than the negative things that have occurred.

"Let your life speak" and "Everything begins with intention" are the two mantras I live by.

My mentors have changed in line with my business objectives. They're helping me build a million-dollar company. I trust them to point out what I'm not doing right in my business but also to show what is possible, especially since I didn't grow up with entrepreneurs in my circle. To have them in my network and know that they are not mystical characters is a blessing. I realize they've developed a strong work ethic; it's really encouraging to me.

Here is my advice to someone looking to build his or her personal brand:

1. Authenticity is key. No point in having a personal brand if it's not who you are.
2. Develop the ability to take constructive criticism. It's hard to see the big picture when you're standing in it. So being able to take feedback from those around you is important.
3. Consistency is essential, especially early on. While you're building your business, you need to be everywhere your audience turns. Your presence needs to be undeniable.

Having a personal brand as an employee is also important. While you have a traditional job, I wouldn't say you're more secure, but you do need to be in a position to have a brand in case something happens. We're moving to a position where people hire names.

People do not want to build you through their company; they want you to come already built. If you're thinking about entrepreneurship, you need a personal brand. Every successful entrepreneur has a personal brand: Steve Jobs, Elon Musk, Oprah, and others like them. If your interests are aligned with your profession, create a blog or write for other people based on your experience; volunteer to speak on panels to position yourself as a thought leader in your industry. Go the extra mile. If you're a female in pharmaceuticals, for example, think of different ways to raise your profile and stand out in your industry.

www.myfabfinance.com
Instagram: @myfabfinance

How to Crush It like a Six-Figure Trailblazer Checklist

Consider these statements to help you crush it:

☐ I continually educate myself on my industry.

☐ I seek out mentors and coaches to help take my business to the next level.

☐ I use video or Facebook Live to engage with my audience.

☐ I show up every day to add value to my community, even when I don't feel like it.

☐ I pitch my business to journalists and bloggers.

PART 3

Taking it to the NEXT LEVEL

You can choose courage, or you can choose comfort, but you cannot choose both.

—Brene Brown, scholar, author, and public speaker.

Claim Your Spot: Become a Thought Leader

When you google yourself, what comes up? Are you seen as one of the best in your industry? If not, think about how you can begin to build your expertise and a stronger online presence. Sharing informative, original content of interest to your audience is a big part of becoming a thought leader in your niche. After a period of time, you will have built enough social proof to demonstrate your credibility.

Consistently add value to your community. Share your views. There are so many ways to share content, including articles, blog posts, videos, and Facebook Live. Take your pick. Make sure your content is unique and in line with your overall brand. There's no point in exclusively sharing other people's content. You're not a journalist! Your audience wants to hear your perspective, so don't be shy about putting your voice out there. But remember, the needs and interests of your audience must prevail over your own. Personal anecdotes will help build a rapport, but you should mix them with other content so it's not all about you.

Stay Ready (So You Don't Need to Get Ready)!

When you're an entrepreneur, customer testimonials will help promote your work without you feeling too Kanye about it. Consistently seek feedback from your customers, and eventually, your brand will sell itself. If you're in the corporate world, don't wait until your annual appraisal to rush around collecting feedback. Get feedback on an on-going basis, so you're ready to shine come review time.

Be Your Own Publicist

Publicity can expose you to a global audience almost over-night. Spend some time doing your own PR. Women are generally less comfortable promoting themselves than men. It's not enough to be good at your job; people must be made aware that you are competent. Self-promotion does not come naturally to most people, but it's a skill that must be mastered.

Marketing consultant Kelly Watson[1] suggests the reason women avoid talking about their achievements is a result of the "four myths of self-promotion":

- The Bitch Myth: "Self-promotion will make me look arrogant."
- The Princess Myth: "If I'm good enough, people will hear about it."
- The Friends and Family Myth: "Others should talk about my accomplishments, not me."
- The Martyr Myth: "You can't control what people think, anyway."

---

1 Kelly Watson, "The Four Myths of Self-Promotion," *Forbes*, June 29, 2010. https://www.forbes.com/2010/06/29/marketing-promotion-small-business-owners-forbes-woman-entrepreneurs-careers-passion.html

Watson goes on to say that "if you don't fully believe in yourself, you'll naturally resist stepping into the spotlight." Do any of these statements sound familiar? If so, it's time to do something about it. Start by thinking about what you want to be known for.

What's Your Story?

In short, what message do you want to share with the world? The best way to do this is through storytelling. One of your most powerful and controllable assets is your personal tale.

Take a moment to consider your personal story. Most of the world's most popular businesses are inseparable from their founder's backstory. Look at the social network behemoth that is Facebook: CEO and founder Mark Zuckerberg's personal history is intricately bonded with his creation. Hone your own personal message until you know it cold and it can form part of your pitch.

What is it about you or your product or service that makes you unique? Most people believe they don't have a story to tell. Wrong. Everyone does! You must master the art of sharing your story in a compelling way.

Your elevator pitch is a great way to share who you are. It must leave people excited about your capabilities. Show your value; otherwise, it's a wasted opportunity.

Before moving to New York from London, I used to shy away from going into detail about my work. When I'd meet people, I'd simply tell them I was a publicist without going into detail. But after becoming my own boss, I realized failing to clearly articulate what I do is a huge missed opportunity. Now when people ask, I fully explain the value I add to my clients.

"I work with female entrepreneurs to help them build powerful personal brands to increase their visibility and propel the growth of their business."

My Story in 30 Seconds

I knew one person when I moved to New York from London in 2012. After working for two years in corporate America, I began to get itchy feet. Slight problem: I was stuck. The limitations of my visa meant if I left the job, I'd have to leave the country. But I knew in my heart that my New York chapter was not over.

I hired a lawyer and began the long, arduous process of applying for a green card. Thankfully, I'd already built a solid portfolio and had spoken at various high-profile events such as Yale University's Women in Leadership conference. Having a strong personal brand proved vital. Within eighteen months I got my green card—a huge accomplishment that meant I could start my business.

Now the above paragraphs may seem like a lot, but reading this through with my PR lens, there are several ways this story can be pitched to journalists at different media outlets to help establish credibility in my niche.

Topics may include

- The struggles of relocating to another country;
- Cultural differences of being a Londoner living in New York;
- Building a personal brand in a new country;
- Networking tips;
- Millennials in the workplace; and
- Building a successful business from nothing.

These are just some of the headlines my story can take. My pitch could work for travel, human resources, and millennial and entrepreneurial publications, among others. Think about your personal story. Create four or five stories, and write an outline for each of them. Which media outlets could you pitch your story outlines to?

Quick Tips to Get Press

Having a reporter in your niche write about you and your business is a great way to share your message with a global audience.

Below are a few tips and tricks that have proven successful for getting press coverage for me and my clients over the years.

Be Interesting!

Your pitch to reporters should whet the reporter's appetite. Lead with the nugget of information most likely to excite the reporter. Demonstrate that you know their beat—a quick Google search should reveal their recent articles. Are they a good fit for your story? If so, write a pitch that is targeted to their interests and to the point.

Jump On the Bandwagon

Keep an eye on the daily news cycle. What eventful news is breaking in your industry? Journalists will likely be looking for spokespeople to comment. How can you connect your expertise to the breaking news?

Build Relationships

Who are the reporters and influencers in your niche? Do some research on them. Create a list, and make a point to build relationships. Start by sharing their content online and commenting on their posts.

Host Your Own Event

Establish authority in your industry through hosting your own event. Colleges and universities are perfect for this, since students are generally keen to learn new things. Pick a topic in your area of expertise. Alternatively, to reach a wider audience, run the event online as a webinar. That way people from all around the world can watch you in action. You can promote it inexpensively across your social media channels.

Write an Article for a Trade Magazine

After working to build your credibility using the strategies outlined, pitch yourself to a trade publication. Pick a popular topic that will resonate with the readers. Send four or five bullet points outlining what your article will cover to the features editor of the magazine. Don't write the article in full until you hear back from the reporter. You don't want to spend time writing an article only for it to be declined, so provide just an overview to begin with.

The Power of Partnerships

> *There is a secret that separates the key person of influence who makes real money and those who look good but still don't make the money they are worth.*
>
> —Daniel Priestley,
> entrepreneur and author.

You will only go so far by yourself. The ultimate cherry on the cake comes through partnerships. Imagine all the people operating in your industry who already have a tribe of raving fans. How great would it be to introduce your product or service to this new audience?

Strategic partnerships will rapidly build your brand awareness and propel you to new audiences. But it must be a win-win partnership, otherwise it won't work. Richard Branson, for instance was able to grow the Virgin brand quickly with over 150 partnerships.

When pitching brands to partner with always focus more on what the brands serve to gain by partnering with you. In the early years of building the My Fab Finance business, Tonya Rapley sought out brands that were complementary to hers.

Who can you can partner with?

There are various partnership deals you can enter to accelerate the growth of your business and personal brand.

Affiliate Partnerships
This type of partnership encourages people to promote products in exchange for a commission. Within the online course space, Amy Porterfield, an online marketing expert, has an affiliate deal with multi-entrepreneur Marie

Forleo to promote her B-School program. Amy promotes B-School to her large audience for a percentage of the courses bought.

Product Partnership

This is where you can team up with a complementary brand or service to create a new, more valuable product. Sammy Aki, a menswear consultant, partners with brands to offer a more comprehensive service to her clients. When considering this type of partnership, think from the perspective of the client. How can you add the most value?

Co-promotion Partnerships

This partnership strategy is where two companies work together to promote a particular product to each other's audience. The co-promotion strategy is a great way to create more buzz and increase sales with less work. Niyc Pidgeon partnered with the United Nations to become a women's ambassador, promoting gender equality and an end to domestic violence against women. Since her mission is to help one million women through positive psychology, there was a clear synergy with the UN's mission, thus the partnership is win-win.

How to Progress with Partnerships

Begin by making a list of the people you need to talk to. Focus on building a relationship first, before asking.

LinkedIn and Instagram, depending on your niche are great places to find relevant contacts. Next, develop a strong pitch. Do thorough research to help ensure the messaging resonates. Pick up the phone to begin putting yourself forward. You'll be surprised how fast things can move, especially if you have already built a solid personal brand.

Partnerships can generate huge rewards. Once they are in place, the possibilities are endless.

Taking It to the Next Level Checklist

Consider these statements to take your personal brand to the next level:

☐ When I google myself, my expertise is clear for all to see.

☐ I get press coverage.

☐ I have a clear idea of five journalists or bloggers in my niche to whom I can pitch.

☐ I host my own events.

☐ I have identified five complementary partners to work with.

USEFUL RESOURCES

www.womenwhoinfluence.club
Free resources, downloads and articles to learn how to build your personal brand and get publicity.

www.canva.com
Free graphic design site for web or print: blog graphics, presentations, Facebook covers, flyers, posters, invitations—you name it!

www.calm.com
Free meditation app for sleep and stress reduction.

www.moleskine.com
Makers of the legendary journals. Inexpensive and useful to write down your ideas.

www.toastmasters.org
International public-speaking and leadership training. A great community for people wanting to improve their ability to deliver engaging talks.

www.ted.com
Tons of inspiring and highly informative talks. Also a great site to visit ahead of your own speaking engagements to learn how to present like a pro.

Stay in touch: www.womenwhoinfluence.club/book

Instagram: @WomenWhoInfluence

Use the hashtag #PersonalBrandBible to share
your photos of the book on social media.

Made in the USA
Columbia, SC
16 July 2018